DIVIDEND INVESTING FOR BEGINNERS

An Effective Guide to Dividend Investing for Passive Income

By
Jerry A. Wood

Disclaimer and Copyright

The author is neither a registered investment, legal or tax advisor, nor a dealer/ broker. All financial and investment opinions expressed in this publication are from the personal experience and research conducted by the author. Although the best efforts have been made to ensure accuracy and timeliness of the information contained within, unintended errors, misprints, and omissions may still occur. The past performance of funds, stocks, and other financial instruments do not necessarily predict future results. When making critical financial and investing decisions, you should do your research and due diligence and/ or seek independent financial advice.

Cover image: Freepik.com. This cover has been designed using resources from Freepik.com.

Table of Contents

Introduction

Dividend investing is just a strategy to buy stocks that are usually issuing dividends as an effort to create a constant stream of passive income. This approach is for the investors that want to be on the stock market for the long term.

Dividend investing is for the very cautious investor, the one that doesn't like to take too many risks. It allows the investor to benefit from the constant stream of passive income from his/her holding. There are plenty of reasons why investors should consider dividend investing.

A major theme of this book is also to take advantage of dividend payments for income and seeking dividend payments that are growth-oriented. So, in the end, you don't need a bank account except for emergency savings. And let me do my duty at this point and encourage you to put a great deal of effort into building a small savings account to help you weather problems that may arise in your life.

If you don't have a savings account or if you do and there's hardly any money in it, I recommend that you make a goal of getting $20,000 into that savings account. Now, you don't have to do that all at once, but set a goal that is at most 24-36 months out, to put regular monthly deposits into your savings account. After that, just leave it alone, unless it's a real emergency.

Thanks for downloading this book. It's my firm belief that it will provide you with all the answers to your questions.

Chapter 1: Dividend Investing Explained

Investing in dividend stocks can be right for you if you are looking for an investment that provides a regular income. Dividend-paying companies regularly distribute a percentage of their profits to investors. Moreover, many dividend stocks in the US are paying investors a fixed amount every quarter, while other companies increase their payouts over time. Hence, it's not unreasonable to expect (after building your portfolio of dividend stocks) a cash stream that resembles an annuity.

Some Companies Pay Dividends, Others Don't

There are several reasons why a company may choose to pass some of its profits as dividends, and another set of reasons why some companies prefer not to issue dividends and instead use all the earnings for growth.

For a stable company with regular earnings that doesn't require reinvestments, dividend payouts can be a good idea because:

- Many investors see dividend payouts as an indicator that the company is strong. It is also a sign that the company has positive projections for earnings in the future that makes the stock more enticing. Remember, higher demand for a company stock will boost its price
- Many investors are looking for a steady income that is linked with dividends, so they will be more likely to purchase the company's stocks.

On the other hand, some companies choose not to issue dividends because of the following reasons:

- Startup companies that are rapidly growing will not issue dividends because it needs to invest as much as possible into their growth
- Established companies also choose not to issue dividends if its directors believe it will do a better job of increasing its share price through reinvestment.
- Some companies choose to temporarily suspend dividends to begin a new project, buy out another company, or repurchase some of their shares.
- Companies that choose to reinvest all their profits, rather than issuing dividends may also think about the expensive cost of new stock issuance. To stay away from raising funds through this channel, they decide to keep the profits.
- The decision to begin paying dividends or to increase a current dividend rate is a huge business decision. Firms that will suddenly cancel or even reduce their current dividend payout could be viewed unfavorably, and the share price may decrease as a result.
-

US companies that historically decided not to pay dividends include Tesla, Biogen, Amazon, Alphabet, and Facebook.

Types of Dividends

A dividend is a cash payout issued by shareholders of a company. But there are different types of dividends, some of which don't involve the payment of cash to stockholders. Below are the different types of dividends:

1. Cash Dividend

Most dividends are considered as cash dividends in the form of electronic transfer or check. The value of the cash dividend will be transferred from the company to the stockholders, instead of the former using it for growth or operations.

If a company decides to issue a cash dividend that is equivalent to the 5 percent of the share price, you can see a resulting loss of 5 percent in the share price. This is caused by economic value transfer.

Another effect of the cash dividend is that the recipients of cash dividends should pay tax on the distribution value, which can lower down its final amount.

However, cash dividends can be beneficial for the investors because it will provide you with regular passive income on your investment on top of the possible appreciation of your capital investment.

Some of these companies that pay cash dividends include Wendy's, Texas Instruments, Home Depot and JPMorgan Chase.

Stock Dividend

A company issues stock dividends to its shareholders without consideration. Most stock dividends are common stocks. When a company issues less than 25% of the total number of outstanding shares, then the transaction is considered as stock dividends. On the other hand, the transaction is regarded as a stock split if it is in a higher proportion of the outstanding shares.

If a company decides to issue a 5 percent stock dividend, it will increase the number of shares by 5 percent. If you are a stockholder of this company, you will be entitled to 1 share for every 20 shares you own, while 1 million shares will net 50,000 additional shares.

However, this doesn't increase the company's value. If the share price of a company is at $10/share, then the value of the company will be at $10 million. After the issuance of the stock dividend, the company's value shall remain the same, but the price will be lower at $9.50 because of the settlement of the stock dividend.

One primary advantage of a stock dividend is that you will have a choice. You may either retain your shares and bet that the company will use the cash to increase its share price, or you may choose to sell some of your shares so you can convert your stocks into cash.

Cash Dividend Vs. Stock Dividend

The cash dividend seems a better choice if you want an automatic reward for placing your investments in specific companies. But this is not always true.

In various ways, it is better for both the shareholder and the company to choose stock dividends at least once a year. A stock dividend is as useful as cash with the extra advantage of not paying taxes upon receipt.

You would be a multi-millionaire today if you were one of the early investors who purchased Microsoft's shares in 1986. If you held 100 shares of this stock at $21 per share, your holding would have increased to 28,000 shares now. This was the reason Bill Gates became the richest man in the world.

One of the main reasons for issuing stock dividends instead of cash dividends could be that in doing so, a company and its stockholders can establish stronger links with investors acquiring more of the company with the extra shares.

As long as they are not bundled with a cash option, stock dividends are considered superior to cash dividends.

Companies that are paying stock dividends are providing their stockholders the option to convert the shares into cash or keep their profit.

There is no other option if you choose the cash dividend.

However, this doesn't mean that cash dividends are not great. The only downside of this dividend is the limit in your options. You can still choose to reinvest your cash dividends into the company via a reinvestment plan.

Meanwhile, choosing stock dividends is not always a better alternative than taking the cash. Remember, the stock market is very unpredictable. The value of shares could drastically be affected by economic turmoil, such as the Great Depression of 1929 and the Global Financial Recession of 2008.

2. Liquidating Dividend

Liquidating dividends are issued when the board of directors of a company decides to return the capital originally paid by stockholders as a dividend. This is usually a negative indicator because it is often paid before the business shuts down.

Companies issuing liquidating dividends may choose to pay the bill in one or several installments. US companies are mandated to issue Form 1099-DIV to all its stockholders that contain all the information about the payout.

Even with several tax benefits, liquidating dividends may not be enough to cover initial investment as the fundamental quality of the company may have significantly plummeted.

3. Scrip Dividend

Scrip dividends are issued by companies who don't have enough funds to issue dividends anytime soon. This type of dividend is a promissory note to pay stockholders at a specific date.

The promissory note creates a note payable and may or may not include interest.

4. Property Dividend

Companies may choose to issue the non-monetary dividend as an alternative to stock or cash payment. This type of property dividend may either include shares of a subsidiary organization or any physical assets that are owned by the company like real estate, equipment, or inventories.

Property dividends are recorded at the market value of the asset distributed. Investors may choose to hold the asset for possible capital gains, but this is usually for the long-term perspective, especially with real estate dividends.

This form of payout scheme is less common compared to the cash or stock dividend system. From a corporate perspective, property dividends could be distributed if the main company doesn't have sufficient cash on hand to distribute significant payouts, or it doesn't want to dilute its existing share position.

Even though these are considered non-cash dividends, property dividends still have a cash value.

How Companies Pay Dividends

Companies usually pay dividends in the form of a check, but some also issue dividends as stock options.

The normal process for dividend payment is a check that is often sent to shareholders a few days after the former dividend date, the date on which the stock begins trading without the declared dividend.

On the other hand, some companies issue additional shares equivalent to the amount of dividend payout. This alternative is known as dividend reinvestment and often provided as a dividend payment option by mutual funds and individual companies.

Take note that dividends are taxable income regardless of the form you received them.

Dividend Reinvestment Plans or DRIPs provide several benefits to investors. If you want to simply add your present equity holdings with any added funds from dividend payments, a plan can simplify the process as opposed to getting the dividend payment in monetary form and then using the money to buy more shares.

In-house reinvestment plans are often commission-free because you don't need to pay brokerage fees. This attribute makes it enticing for small investors because commission fees are proportionately bigger for smaller stock purchases.

Another advantage of a reinvestment plan is that some companies are offering shareholders the opportunity to buy added shares in cash at a lower price.

The price reduction can go between 1 and 10% on top of the additional benefit of waived broker fees. So, you can buy more stock holdings at a discounted price over investors who buy shares in cash through brokerage fees.

When to Expect Dividend Payout

If a company decides to issue dividends, stockholders are notified through a press release, and the news will also be reported via major stock quoting services for easier reference.

Upon the announcement, a schedule will be set, or a record date, which means all stockholders on this date will be entitled to the payout. The day after the record date is known as ex-date, which refers to the date that the stock starts trading ex-dividend.

Hence, if you acquire shares on an ex-date, you will not be eligible for the payout. Usually, the payable date is 30 days after the record date.

When the payable date arrives, the company will deposit the dividends with the Depository Trust Company (DTC). Payouts are then distributed by the DTC to brokerage companies around the globe where stockholders are holding the shares of the company.

In turn, the brokerage firms will deposit cash payouts to their client accounts or process reinvestment plans upon the instruction of the shareholder.

Preferred Stocks Vs. Common Stocks

Preferred stockholders are usually prioritized when it comes to claiming the company's earnings and assets. This covers the issuance of dividends, wherein preferred shareholders are paid before common stockholders.

Advantages of Dividend Investing

Somehow, receiving dividends is like getting interest on your bank savings. It can be quite nice but doesn't provide the thrill from betting on the rise and fall of share prices. People love the exhilarating experience, especially when prices are soaring. However, if you are a conservative investor, dividend stocks provide several benefits over-investing in non-dividend stocks.

Below are some of the reasons why it is beneficial for investors to choose dividend stocks:

1. Passive Income

Dividends from stocks can provide you a regular flow of passive income than you may choose to reinvest or spend. This is the main attribute that attracts many retirees who are looking for supplemental income.

2. Lower Risk

Dividend stocks have less volatility in share price, and they usually have a lower risk-to-reward ratio. Because of these attributes, dividend stocks can experience a minimal decline in the share price during a market downturn. Lower volatility can also temper the appreciation of the share price during the market recovery.

3. More Stable Companies

Dividend stocks are often paid by companies that are more stable. Startup companies usually don't pay dividends as they need to reinvest most of their profits to sustain their growth. The board of directors will only decide to pay dividends only when the company has achieved a sustainable level of success. Meanwhile, the need to distribute dividends will compel the management to be more responsible.

4. Hedge Against Inflation

Inflation is the main enemy of earnings from stock investments. A moderate inflation rate could take a huge bite out of your profits. Even if you earn a 10% return, a 3% inflation can result in only 7% earnings. Dividends can offset this loss. As companies increase their prices because of inflation, they will earn more money and pay higher dividends.

5. Baby Boomer Boost

The price for dividend stocks could go up as the demand for it will increase because of baby boomers reaching retirement and seeking sources of supplemental income. While this is somewhat of an expert projection, it is still a projection, and there's no guarantee that this will really happen. However, the probability of this happening is much higher.

6. Positive Returns in Bear Markets

Companies that are paying dividends will still pay their dues even in bear markets when share prices are dropping or flat. The dividends can help in offsetting any loss from a fall in share prices, and there are cases that the results are even positive.

7. Two Ways to Make a Profit

The returns from the dividend stocks could increase when companies pay dividends, and when the share prices increase. The only way you can earn positive returns from non-dividend stocks is via appreciation of share price - selling high and buying low.

8. Cash to Purchase More Shares

Once you purchase a certain number of shares of a non-dividend company, you can obtain that certain number of shares. If you like to acquire more shares, you need to use your own money to buy additional units. If you invest in dividend stocks, you can buy additional shares through reinvestment of all or some of your dividends. There is no need to use your money in your pocket to buy more shares. Most investors are also enrolled in special programs, which allow them to reinvest their dividends automatically.

9. Ownership Retention and Profit Collection

Among the most disappointing attributes of owning shares of non-dividend stock is that all your profits are locked in the investment. You can only access your profits by selling some of your shares. Through dividend stocks, you can retain ownership of the company while still collecting your returns.

While dividend stocks pose less risk compared to non-dividend stocks, they also carry some risk and may not be suitable for all types of investors. Aside from the benefits, you should also understand the drawbacks of dividend investing. This will help you decide if this type of stock market investment is really right for you.

Each time you sign an investment agreement with an intermediary such as a mutual fund manager or a broker, you will usually read a lengthy disclaimer about the results not guaranteed. To put this simply, you may earn money from your investments today, but there is no certainty that it will be the same case tomorrow. Just like any other kind of investment, dividend investing also carries some risk.

Disadvantages of Dividend Investing

1. High Dividend Payout Risk

Investing in stocks with a high dividend payout ratio comes with risk. Take note that the company's dividend payout ratio reflects how much of its profits are used to reinvest in growth, pay its debts, serve as cash reserve versus how much is being paid to shareholders.

It can be a delicate balancing act for most companies to figure out the percentage of its profits to allocate for dividends. They surely like to entice and retain investors with high payouts but also need to keep enough of their earnings to support further growth and, at the same time, maintain their capacity to raise the dividend in the future.

In reality, once the dividend payout ratio of a company becomes too high for sustainability, this can force the business to reduce or cancel payouts altogether.

2. Dividend Policy Changes

Dividend policy refers to the company's plan for figuring out its amount for dividends and any possible increases based on projected earnings. Once a company makes changes to the policy, specifically those that result in reducing or canceling payouts, it will have an adverse effect on its share price.

Based on the clientele effect theory, the price of a stock is strongly connected to the reaction of investors to policy changes of the company. So when these changes happen, many investors will purchase or sell their company shares.

When a company is forced to cancel its dividends for any reason, you may lose your passive income.

3. Double Taxation

Another disadvantage of investing in dividend stocks is that the payouts are subject to double taxation.

First, you need to pay tax when you receive your payouts because the company issuing the dividends from its net profit has to pay tax on its yearly earnings. These earnings generate the dividend payments of the company.

Second, you need to pay tax again as you receive the payouts as personal income that you have earned over the course of a certain tax year.

Therefore, you are paying tax twice as an individual and as a part-owner of a company.

In general, dividend investing is less risky compared to non-dividend stock investing. However, before you can maximize the returns from this type of investment, you need to be very familiar with both the benefits and drawbacks before you buy your first shares.

Managing Risks in Dividend Investing

There is always a risk in stock market investing due in part to its unpredictable and variable nature. That being said, there are several factors that can increase risk, some are within your control, and some are not.

Even though we cannot eliminate the risk, it is still possible to minimize our exposure by becoming more aware of the factors that influence market behavior. As a savvy investor, you can manage the risks in dividend investing by dealing with factors that you can control.

1. Diversifying Your Investments

You must never invest all your money in one company stock regardless of how promising the business is. Its competitors may dominate the market. The management may be corrupt or incompetent. Or the firm or its whole industry may lose the favor of investors for any reason. These are beyond your control.

The good thing is that you have absolute control over where you want to pour your money. You can greatly minimize the risk by spreading your stock investments in different stocks.

2. Minimize Human Error

Human error is the largest risk factor with dividend investing, and it may result from the following:

- Lack of knowledge
- A misaligned investment strategy and investment goals
- Insufficient research and analysis
- Using emotions over logic in choosing stocks
- Failure to keep track of market conditions
- Allowing panic and fear influence investment decisions

Doing your due diligence is the best way to eliminate human error. You certainly know the risk involved in not being prepared if you have taken an exam you have not studied for. Aside from the unsettling feeling of having not knowing the right answers, you will experience panic that will not help your situation.

3. Use Reason Over Emotion

The Efficient Market Hypothesis is one of the prevailing theories about the mechanics behind the stock market. This hypothesis describes investors as logical people who are capable of understanding all available information in the market to make reasonable decisions for maximum profits. However, most people are not logical or rational.

Many investors are buying stocks based on advice from their family or friends and sometimes from people they don't know. Some investors buy or sell their stocks because of what they heard over the news or because a new company is making a product they adore, and they are sure that it will be a big hit in the market. They know nothing about the history of the stock, its management, or the company as a whole. To effectively manage the risks in dividend investing, it is best to avoid these three major emotions: Love, Fear, and Greed.

Love:

You must never fall in love with your investments. Remember, these are lifeless things that are not capable of loving you back. But, interestingly, they can betray you and hurt you.

Some investors are so in love with the company they hold stocks in that they refuse to sell even when indicators show that the company's inherent value has deteriorated, and the share price is falling. You need to bail out when a stock decline sharply. Review your stocks regularly and scrutinize each investment on its recent performance. If it is not contributing to your portfolio's growth, you can sell your shares, which you can easily do because stocks are very liquid.

Fear:

Investors who experienced losing money in the stock market are susceptible to fear that it paralyzes them from taking any action. Rather than taking on some risk with high potential investments, they are putting their money in safe investments with low rates of return.

Greed:

Greed is the opposite of fear. Most investors who have made much money in the stock market would usually want more. Some investors are vulnerable to the bandwagon effect, pouring their money into the "hottest" companies and industries. This inflates a bubble that will eventually burst. Greedy investors usually tend to invest in instruments they don't fully understand, or they can't afford and then fall into the trap of increasing their investments to recover their losses.

Chapter 2: Rules of Dividend Investing

Dividend investments, just like any other niche, comes with its own set of rules. Think of these rules as shortcuts to avoid making common mistakes. These rules are backed by academic research and principles from some of the world's greatest investors. Mind you, don't think of these rules as infallible since there will always be an exception. Nevertheless, it's good to integrate these rules into your everyday investment decisions.

1. Always Go for Quality

Long-term orientation is one of the best advantages an investor could ever have. It is a rule to invest in businesses that have stability, profit, and a proven track record showing growth. Why should you go for a mediocre business when you can invest in a high-quality business? As a financial rule, you should rank stocks by both their dividend and corporate history length, and the longer they are, the better.

2. The Bargain Principle

It is a rule to invest in businesses that pay you the most dividends for the cash you invest. Remember, the higher the dividend yield, the better. In addition to this, avoid investing in overpriced securities. You should only deal with stocks trading below a decade historical average valuation multiple, which is the average value of stocks calculated over ten years.

3. Always Play Safe

Avoid businesses that payout all their income as dividends, as this means that the company has no margin of safety, and dividends can be reduced at any time.

4. Reinvest Your Dividends

This is one rule you must never break. The power of reinvesting your dividends cannot be undermined. Putting your dividends back to work can do wonders for your portfolio.

What's more? You can make use of reinvestment programs, which often enable you to reinvest your payouts automatically without paying a commission fee.

5. Understand Your Tax Laws

Get familiar with the tax structure for dividends and take note of any changes resulting from a new company or government policies.

6. Don't Make Dividends Your Only Priority

Dividends are an indispensable part of investing. However, dividends are not the all-mighty metric to abide by. Investors need to pay attention to different fundamentals that are often at play in investments. Fundamentals like profits, price actions, and earning growths are just a few of the features you need to pay attention to. Remember to look beyond high-dividend yields and ensure you understand the company's growth pattern and future prospects.

7. Watch Out for Value Traps

Many investors jump at seemingly lucrative stocks without realizing that they are value traps. A value trap is a phenomenon where dividend yield is increasing, and stock prices are reducing. When faced with this phenomenon, most investors think they've hit the jackpot. However, they fail to realize that the stock prices were reducing for a legitimate reason. So how can you detect this trap before it is too late? Here's the first sign to watch out for. When you see a company that pays out far more than its peers in the sector or market index, this indicates a value trap. In addition to this, falling cash flows with stable yields also show a value trap.

8. Always Look Out for Special Dividends

One of the perks of dividend investments is the ability of corporations to initiate a one-time dividend payout. When looking for stocks to purchase, these one-time dividend payouts often mislead investors. During one-time dividend payments, a company's stock might seem rosier than usual. A good example is Microsoft (MSFT), who issued a one-time dividend payment in 2004, which was a sharp contrast to the regular dividend payouts. Microsoft's regular dividend payouts varied from $0.3 to $0.5, while the one-time dividend payout was a whopping $3 per share. Many resources calculate the one-time dividend payment as an annual yield. If we were to include the special dividend payout, Microsoft's yearly return for 2004 would have been 13.78 percent, instead of the 0.38 percent payout from regular dividends. As you can see, the figure was enough to confuse investors who hadn't checked and analyzed the yield statistics.

9. Use the Survival of the Fittest Principle

Sell your stocks when your dividend payouts are reduced or cut short—it's that simple. Research carried out between 1972 and 2017 showed that stocks that cut or reduced their dividend payouts had a 0 percent recovery. If your dividends are reduced or stopped, this goes against the principles of generating passive income. It is the opposite of what we are aiming for. Any business that cuts its dividends has lost its competitive advantage. Therefore, you want to reinvest the proceeds of your sale into a more profitable stock.

Chapter 3: Building a Dividend Portfolio

When it comes to investing in any form of the market, prior knowledge benefits investors the most in their efforts to save for retirement as they work and grow. No one should try to play a sport without having knowledge of the game. Otherwise, they will not be adequately prepared and will be quickly overtaken by the sharks in the water.

When building a portfolio of dividend stocks, an investor needs to know how to build an income and how it will help cover those financial needs long after you had that retirement celebration at the office, where everyone congratulated you for your years of service. This doesn't mean you need to find a get-quick-rich scheme because investing in dividends is something you should plan to have working for you for a few decades—which requires knowing where to start and how to set up a dividend portfolio.

Knowing the Risks of Inflation

Keep in mind that the possibility of the market's risk of inflation—a sustained increase of the prices on goods and services within the economy over an extended period of time—can affect different companies in various ways, depending on how much of an impact those higher costs have on where you invest.

There existed some risks that need to be kept in mind and weighed against each other when making those investment decisions. Experts usually subject themselves to both inflation, and the market risk involved, and the amount they are involved vary depending on how much they diversify their dividend portfolio. It's a challenging dilemma for everyone who invests while trying to find a dependable income for the long road ahead.

For example, a $1-million portfolio with a 5 percent rate usually provides an investor with about $50,000 each year in income that can protect an investor from the aforementioned market risk. But let's say that an inflation rate of 3 percent causes the investor to only have about $35,000 of buying power about twelve years later. If you add a tax rate of about 30 percent, that $50,000 then becomes about $25,000 at the end of twelve years.

Benefits of Market Growth

So then, why would you choose to invest in dividends? Just about every portfolio on the market has its own set of risks. In essence, even non-guaranteed dividends and other economic risks like the one mentioned a few graphs above where there was a healthy dividend-paying list of equities with a 4 percent yield.

Usually, these have a payout that increases at least 3 percent each year and covers the inflation rate, possibly growing 5 percent annually over those same twelve years. If the latter were to happen, then that $50,000 you started with would grow to about $90,000 each year but would be about $62,000 after the planned 3 percent inflation rate. Let's say there is a 15 percent tax (which is always something that can change later on). That makes the amount worth about $53,000.

When a portfolio combines both of those methods, it could defend itself against inflation and market fluctuations. Being able to have a diverse portfolio that includes stocks and bonds is an excellent way to make a dependable income that won't be affected too much by the potential dividend hazards.

Remember to Keep Safety in Mind

Just as you were told by your mom to look both ways before crossing a street, you want to avoid any risks before starting to invest in your dividend portfolio. One of those steps requires establishing criteria—that means having to do some homework on any companies that you are considering buying shares in and then waiting until you see a price that is perfect for your investment situation.

You shouldn't rush to pick a company because if it doesn't feel right, you can always wait until you see the price hits a mark that feels more comfortable. By doing this, life can be a lot easier. One example is to wait until finding some excellent blue-chip stocks that feature balance sheets that offer a 4 or 5 percent yield—sometimes more.

Even if you're playing it safe, there are still plenty of risks to look out for—many of them are avoidable as long as an investor makes the proper choices. One example is a yield trap. When companies have larger yields but don't offer much in terms of fundamental health, they tempt investors. Yet, they are not able to provide guaranteed stability. Sure, it looks great at the moment but can lead to becoming a cut in the dividend returns.

Steps to Building a Dividend Portfolio

1. **Create Diversity in Your Portfolio with At Least Twenty-five Solid Stock Options**

This isn't about trying to end up with King Solomon's gold by starting with nothing. Smart investors remain focused on the long-term goal of having money to fund an income during retirement, and that takes time and patience. Receiving dividends should be the focus and not just stock growth without having to accept a company's risk.

2. **Diversity among Multiple Industries**

The right choice means not putting all of your beans in one single pot. For example, if all of your stocks come from different oil companies, it would be a shame if the price per barrel fell as much as $10 or more and would make a negative impact on your dividends. One way of avoiding that dreaded dividend cut is to spread your selections out.

3. Financial Stability Is More Important than Growth

If an investor had an option C on the exam, they would select that one for "both A and B." Such is a difficult decision to make, so the priority of the investor is to focus on having more dependability so that your company will provide dividends that increase over time rather than relying on the opportunity of sudden growth. This can be done by keeping an eye on each company you may potentially invest in by watching their credit ratings. The Value Line Investment Survey usually grades these stocks from A++ and down to the Ds and focus on stocks with A ratings for the least amount of risk.

Examples of companies with financial stability include:
- Target Corp has a market cap of $41 billion, a 27% payout ratio, a PEG ratio of 1.3, a forward P/E of 12.9, and a 2.3% current dividend yield.
- Caterpillar Inc CAT has a market cap of $57 billion, a forward P/E of 8.3, a PEG ratio of 0.51, a 2.4% dividend yield, and a 21% payout ratio.
- Visa Inc has a market cap of $87 billion, a forward P/E of 18.3, a PEG ratio of 1.1, a 0.7% dividend yield, and a 15% payout ratio.
- Dover Corporation has a market cap of $10 billion, a forward P/E of 10.5, a PEG ratio of 1.21, a 2.3% dividend yield, and a 27% payout ratio.
- Aflac Incorporated has a market cap of $30 billion, a forward P/E of 6.6, a PEG ratio of 0.61, a 3% dividend yield, and a 24% payout ratio.

4.   Focus on Companies That Have a History of Raising Their Dividends

Here's an example of what you should look for to insert into your dividend portfolio. Bank of America had a dividend yield of about 4 percent in the early part of 1995, which means forty-seven cents were distributed to each share. But there was purchase back then of about $11.20 per share that led to a dividend in 2006 of $2.12. That means the investor earned about 18.9 percent above the stock's original purchase. One place to find these types of companies is by looking through the list of S&P's "Dividend Aristocrats"—which has seen dividend increases for twenty-five consecutive years—and Mergent's "Dividend Achievers"—which are on a current ten-year streak.

5.   Look for Companies That Have Modest Payout Ratios

Those ratios are calculated from the dividends as a percentage of the total earnings. If a ratio is 60 percent or less, it means the company has a lot less wiggle room when there could be some unforeseeable trouble down the road. It's best to invest in a company that has a plan for what to do to protect their shareholders in case of any economic crisis.

- Target Corp has a 27% payout ratio and a 2.3% current dividend yield.
- Caterpillar Inc CAT has a 2.4% dividend yield and a 21% payout ratio.
- Visa Inc has a 0.7% dividend yield and a 15% payout ratio.
- Dover Corporation has a 2.3% dividend yield and a 27% payout ratio.
- Aflac Incorporated has a 3% dividend yield and a 24% payout ratio.

6.   Reinvest What You Earn from Your Dividends

By putting the money earned into investments well in advance of when you may need the money for that retirement, the dividends could result in a very surprising amount of growth that calls for less effort from the part of the investor.

The Biggest Mistakes to Avoid When Growing Your Portfolio

A big reason why dividends are looking more and more attractive to investors these days is that the yields and bonds are stressfully low, and investors who are looking to plan for their eventual retirement are looking towards dividend-paying stocks for a more dependable income that builds efficiently over a longer period of time.

Dividend investing has become a popular strategy during a time where fixed-income is falling into lows that haven't been hit before, and the baby boomer generation is preparing to enter the world of retirement.

That's not to say there isn't any sort of pitfalls, as with anything in the stock market during tough economic times. There are a number of catches in the face of all of the good things that dividend portfolios bring.

Chasing Those Big Yield Goals

The stocks with the largest dividend payments do not always provide the best return overall for investors. That's because those higher rates cannot remain at a sustainable level for more than a year, which can leave a company that was enjoying the ride up on the roller coaster with a sudden "unexpected" drop—this leads into companies having to make dividend cuts and a funds shortage that all lead into a difficulty in any future growth.

That's why many experts recommend using the dividend payout ratios in addition to the yields so that you don't depend on one aspect as much. It also gives you a chance to avoid those dangerous yield spikes.

They recommend having a ratio with a payout anywhere between 30 and 60 percent that is in a perfect position for the company to guarantee providing consistent cash distribution amongst all of their shareholders. At the same time, that percentage is not too high to allow for funds to be reinvested for additional internal growth, which is also known as the utilization of the power of compounding interest.

Relying on Overly Mechanical Investment Plans

These strategies often overlook basic shifts and dividend policy updates, which could create a problem for an investor's dividend income flow. This has happened a few times in Europe where some of the telecommunication companies that paid via dividends had higher yields that had increased beyond 100 percent—which, as mentioned earlier, is a warning sign that things are about to go down because what goes up must come down.

Ignoring a Variety of Growth Factors

Successful investors have to look at and evaluate not only the dividend yields that each company has paid out but also what the company's potential is for both growth and appreciation—growth is what allows someone to be able to have more paid out to them over a longer amount of time, going ahead to help them sustain a livable income after they join the retirement community.

For example, let's imagine that an investor has a portfolio with $1 million and wants to withdraw about $50,000 per year for expenses, like home, food, etc. If the investor earns about 3 percent in total returns, less than half of the starting balance will remain after twenty years. Another ten years later, that same investor earning only 3 percent would be close to running out. Now, if that same person were able to grow their returns to about 7 percent, they would have savings of about $3 million after that same thirty-year period.

Showing Favoritism to the Home Market

There are many options overseas in other countries that have a booming economy that is paying dividends that have higher averages, which are obviously more favorable to investors and sometimes provide better options than in your country.

Investing in the global market has become a very important factor in being able to diversify a portfolio by including the industries in those fast-growing markets. For example, people are starting to move cloud operations overseas to African countries because the demand is growing there—i.e., Amazon and VMware.

In twenty years, those markets have increased their shares of the world economy and account for about 47 percent of the world's gross domestic product.

Focused Toward Those Blue Chips

Investors sometimes claim there's more safety in having those larger dividend stocks, but they also cost more to buy shares and won't offer as much in return as they once did than the ones that are smaller or middle of the road in capsize. Those larger companies usually offer a liquidity advantage but still don't offer a lot of opportunities to see increased dividend yield.

Investor demand has risen so much that those blue-chip stocks are becoming too costly to even consider as options for a diverse and successful portfolio.

Following What Everyone Else Is Doing

There are a lot of dividend funds that are driven by the indexes that can create what is called benchmark-hugging, where portfolios are overexposed to those larger name companies and stocks while not providing as much attention to the smaller companies that might have a better set of opportunities.

Giving Macro Factors More Weight

There's always going to be plenty of risks when it comes to any form of investing. It's inevitable as there are emerging markets that provide some intriguing potential, especially among troubled nations with possible booms within Europe, the Middle East, and Africa. Those regions may provide a large sum of international revenue gains and local operations that are less likely to be affected by macro trends.

For example, the stocks in the European market aren't being valued as highly due to the current crisis, which causes doubt for investors. But there is still a chance to find some stronger companies that offer dividend payments in that part of the world that could provide some potential gains to help your portfolio.

Chapter 4: High Yield Investment

In dividend stock investing, many investors are following the high dividend yield strategy. This particular strategy could result in large cash income, usually from slow-growth companies that have a substantial cash volume to finance dividend payouts.

However, the unnecessary focus on income alone often obscures the important reality that long-term stock dividend investment is based on the total return of a portfolio, which includes both capital and income growth.

This scenario raises two important questions:
1. How does its total-return performance compare to the profits of other potential stock-option strategies?
2. With a focus on income, how has the total profit of a high-dividend yield strategy fared in comparison to the overall market?

Take note that a high-dividend yield strategy is a systematic approach in buying and holding stocks wherein the dividend is high relative to the share price. As such, this is a strategy that prefers stock valuation because this it's actually the low price of the stock in relation to the dividend, which mainly causes the high yield.

But a high-dividend yield strategy is just one form of strategy in dividend investing, which can help you in selecting stocks. There is also considerable proof and theoretical foundation that value stocks can outperform both market and growth stocks in the long run. In this perspective, the "yield" premium that is linked to high-dividend strategies really refers to the value premium.

Other strategies focus on stocks based on high earnings or high cash flow relevant to price as well as the high book value of equity that is relevant to market value.

One possible explanation for the minimal return of the high-dividend yield stocks compared to stocks chosen via other value metrics is that dividend stocks are usually sourced from bigger companies.

Companies that are not issuing dividends are not included in the list. Therefore, a high-dividend yield strategy foregoes to a higher degree the available return premium available from investing in smaller companies.

Stocks that are chosen on the basis of high profits often demonstrate strong performance. This value strategy could purchase non-dividend-payment of growth companies that are not included in the list and also companies that are generating enough revenues but have reduced their dividend payouts, or they are temporarily suspended.

It is important to take note that no single value strategy could outperform consistently over shorter time frames. Therefore, the diversifying strategy can be beneficial at this point, especially for investors who are a bit impatient.

One major advantage of choosing high-dividend stocks is that they are less volatile in the market. But value stocks based on either cash flow or earnings had modestly higher risk-adjusted profits compared to high-dividend yield strategy.

A high-dividend strategy could result in less stock turnover compared to a strategy that is based on earnings or cash flow, and in this case, it can drastically lower capital gains taxes.

But a strategy that is based on high book-to-market can also decrease turnover and potential capital gains taxes. In general, with a focus on consistent and significant taxable income generation, a high-dividend strategy is not tax-efficient, especially in countries with higher dividend tax rates compared to the US.

Remember, a high-dividend yield strategy has several advantages for dividend investors. This is easy to understand and usually attractive to the innate desire of investors to hold on to their shares. Stocks selected using high-dividend yield strategy are often powerful enough to outperform the market with less volatility.

But if we base this on absolutes, its returns have affected other value strategies. Using the risk-adjusted perspective, the lower volatility can come at the cost of lower returns.

High-dividend yield strategy may not be applicable to wealthy investors or high-income earners. This strategy could trigger unnecessary income that created unnecessary tax drag on the accumulation of wealth.

In summary, investors, especially those that are subject to taxes, might be better off creating a cash flow stream using a systematic withdrawal program from an investment portfolio that attracts higher returns from other values strategies instead of depending solely on a high-dividend yield strategy.

The Advantages of Selecting High-Dividend Yield Stocks

The majority of dividend-paying stocks are in defensive sectors that are poised to sustain economic crises with less volatility. More often than not, dividend-paying companies have significant amounts of cash. Hence, these are established companies with better prospects in the long-term.

Dividend Yields as Regular Cash Stream

Bear in mind that the dividend yield is a financial metric that will help you figure out how much per share a company is paying out per annum in the dividend. This is expressed in percentage.

As a review, you can calculate the dividend yield by taking the yearly dividend per share divided by the price for each share. This will provide a percentage as the dividend yield, as the majority of companies are issuing dividends every quarter.

Dividends can provide a regular source of income for stock investors. You can use this passive revenue to spend or reinvest back in stocks. This is a common practice in the industry.

Investors who are about to retire or are already in retirement usually choose dividend stocks as a source of revenue as long as these stocks are less volatile.

Dividend-paying stocks will allow you to make money in two methods:
- Stock price appreciation
- Distributions issued by the company

The majority of the companies that are issuing stocks have dividend reinvestment plans, which allow investors to use dividends in purchasing more shares in the company.

This will allow you to gradually build a bigger position in a company in the long run. Many companies are not taking commissions for these added shares. Some are even offering discounts.

Companies are offering reinvestment plans because they take advantage of having a base of long-term investors who are actively involved in the future of the business.

Dividend Stocks Are Based in Defensive Sectors

The majority of the companies that are paying dividends are in defensive industries, which are seen as non-cyclical. These companies are not dependent on bigger economic cycles.

Defensive stocks can withstand economic instability, and they are generally less volatile compared to the overall market. This can be a great thing for investors who are risk-averse. These stocks can pay more than investors can receive from conservative securities such as bonds. Hence they are great additions to investment portfolios.

Typical defensive sectors include healthcare, pharmaceutical, utility and housing, and food industries. Even during financial uncertainty, people still need to buy food products and keep the lights on.

Regardless of the status of the economy, people still get sick and require medical care. Healthcare stocks such as Pfizer are usual favorites of investors who love high-dividend stocks.

Established Companies

The majority of companies that are paying dividends are already established companies with well-performing stocks. They have the capacity to distribute dividends to investors because they have a substantial cash reserve. For this reason, they are good stocks to include in your portfolio. Examples of such companies are Coca-Cola and Procter & Gamble that pay 3.5% and 3.95% dividends per year.

In the long run, established companies perform better. Based on a stock analysis published by Forbes in 2015, dividend-paying stocks have shown better performance since

1927. The average growth of dividend-paying stocks is 10.4% compared to the 8.5% annual growth of non-dividend-paying stocks.

Dividend-paying stocks are also less volatile. The average deviation for dividend-paying stocks is 18%, while non-dividend-paying stocks are at 30%.

The Downsides of High Yield Dividend Stocks

The primary risks of high yield dividend stocks include interest rate risk and the inability to make dividend payments. High yield dividend stocks could be remarkable opportunities for savvy investors who can earn a substantial amount from their investments while waiting for the prospect of stock appreciation. Hence, it is crucial to perform proper and deeper due diligence to make sure that dividend payouts are possible.

Remember, a high yield dividend strategy works by choosing stocks that have strong balance sheets and managed by a well-experienced and skilled management team. There are instances that companies with great records of issuing payouts encounter short-term problems or poor market conditions that cause temporary hiccups. This can temporarily raise the dividend yield, which creates opportunities for savvy investors.

Remember, stocks are often affected by the performance of the underlying business as well as the interest rates. If interest rates increase, dividends could become less attractive to investors, which results in equity outflows and selling of stocks.

Many high dividend stocks are in consumer staples, master limited partnerships, utilities, and real estate investment trusts (REITs). Huge cap indexes such as S&P 100 and Dow Jones also contain a lot of high dividend stocks.

High Dividend as an Indicator of Company Distress

Although high dividends are typically attractive to investors, some are actually considered as fool's gold. In some instances, a high dividend may indicate that a company is experiencing distress. You may lose your investment during dividend cuts, or stock price falls if you only choose stocks solely on the basis of the dividend.

The stock market is a forward-looking market and usually doesn't account for the underlying problems of a company. This can make the dividend more enticing for investors.

Let's say that CGF Inc is trading at $50 and issues a $2.50 yearly dividend. Hence, we have a 5% dividend yield. Some movement in the market could result in a loss in earnings capacity, and the share price of the company falls to $25. This is a 50% loss. In the case of dividends, they are not automatically ceased. Hence, on the surface, some investors may see that the yield on CGF stock is now at 10 percent.

But this high dividend yield is only temporary as the same factors that caused the fall of the share price would most likely lead to a decrease in a dividend. In other scenarios, the company may choose to keep the dividend to reward loyal stockholders. Hence, you should not ignore the need to look into the operations and the financials of the company. This will help you determine if the dividend payouts are sustainable.

Some important factors to scrutinize are the status of the company's overall financial health, management's strategy, increases and decreases, historical dividend schedules, historical payout ratio, and free cash flow.

Many of the best dividend-paying companies are usually blue chips in the sector with a stable record of generating revenue and income growth over several quarters and years.

This reputation and credibility usually lend itself to the stable underlying fundamentals that are associated with most companies that are paying dividends.

With this, there will always be new players entering into the mix and companies who are starting to struggle with their dividend payout. Hence, it is crucial to maintain steadfast due diligence.

Risk of Interest Rate

Dividend yields are often being compared to the risk-free rate of return that typically increases in scenarios where the government is implementing stricter financial policies.

As a result, many investors assess dividend and dividend investments in relation to this metric instead of an absolute basis. If the interest rates increase, it could lead to outflows in high dividend yield stocks and may also cause stock prices to decrease. Significant changes in interest rates could be a catalyst for some market movements and possibly result in a bear market. Hence, this is a crucial factor to follow for different investing decisions.

The US government has been increasing interest rates since 2015. The stricter policy is affecting nearly a decade of bullish returns of the stock market. This has also been aligned with increasing inflation, improving the economy, and recovery of the labor market.

This year may be a good time to consider some of the best high dividend stocks and reallocate some investments. This will allow you to take advantage of a higher risk-free rate in liquid cash savings as well as short-term bonds.

Chapter 5: Taxation

Let's face it; most of us don't know much of anything about how our complex tax code is going to be applied when it comes to the stock market and to dividends. If you're a beginning investor, that is definitely true. The first advice that should be given is that if you build up a large portfolio of stocks, you're going to need to use a professional accountant. But having some understanding of the general rules will help as well. You don't want to get into a situation where taxes end up cutting into your profits.

Ordinary versus Qualified Dividends

The first thing to be aware of is the difference between ordinary and qualified dividends. The kinds of dividends that we've been talking about in this book are ordinary dividends. That means that the income from them is, well, ordinary. In other words, the proceeds are taxed as ordinary income.

Tax Forms

The dividends that you get from an investment in dividend stock will be reported on Form 1099-DIV. If you are getting dividend payments from an s-corporation or trust, they will be reported on a Form K-1. Note that investments in vehicles like an MLP will generate a K-1.

Dividends that you reinvest

Unfortunately, the geniuses in Congress didn't see that it was fit to prevent this in the interest of promoting investment, but dividends that you reinvest are still subject to tax, so you have to report any dividends that you receive on your tax return and pay taxes for ordinary income on them.

Example: You earned $25,000 in dividends, but you reinvested them buying more shares. You still have to pay the tax on them. Like the example above, they are more than

$1,500, and so, you need to report them on schedule B of your 1040.

Some tricks to lower your tax burden

If you have an individual retirement account, your money in the account is allowed to grow tax-free. One downside is that the wise old men of Congress limit how much you can invest in an individual retirement account to around $5,500 -6,500 per year depending on age. However, there is a nice trick you can use with dividends inside the individual retirement account. You can use the account to buy dividend earning stocks. Then, when the dividends are paid, they are paid inside your IRA. That means that they are tax-free, and you can reinvest them inside the IRA. Keep in mind that when the money is taken out of your IRA after you retire, if you have a traditional IRA, you're going to have to pay taxes on it at that time (a Roth IRA means you pay taxes on the money now, but the money is tax-free later when you withdraw it).

So, the procedure to avoid paying taxes on dividends is:
- Open an IRA or use an employer retirement account like a 401k
- Buy dividend stocks inside the retirement account
- Reinvest the dividends inside the retirement account
- That way you won't face taxes on the dividends

The same trick can be used to massively grow your retirement accounts using covered calls. So, you buy shares inside the IRA, and then sell covered calls with the IRA account. The odds are good that most of the time, the options aren't going to be exercised. So, you make, say, $2,500 profit a month selling covered calls, and it's inside your IRA, and it's going to be tax-free since the account is allowed to grow tax-free.

Then you use the funds from your covered calls to keep buying more shares. So, although you're only limited to putting in a relatively small amount each year after you've built up a few hundred shares, you can start earning money from selling covered calls and reinvesting the dividends. Then, when you start pulling money out of the IRA when you've retired, you will pay taxes on the money at that time.

Conclusion

It's safe to say that there's a reason that dividends are very popular among the investment community, and if there were a perfect way for them to work, it would be the slow and steady approach—rather than the one where the investor is hoping to find one big gold mine.

There are plenty of options, and because the market offers plenty to choose from, it's a big reason why so many investors will establish a diverse portfolio. Those are the two main keys to success for the investor who is about to get started in the world of dividend investing.

Successful investors plan accordingly. They are not quick at making decisions in regard to selling stocks when they notice a slight decline in the share price. They focus on long term where they will reap great benefits after several years of waiting — which will yield a dependable income to enjoy when you are retired from the workforce.

I hope this book was enjoyable and full of knowledge for you. If you benefited from the information, I would appreciate an honest review.

About the Author

Jerry A. Wood is the pen name of a Certified Project Manager with over 15 years' experience in the tech and finance industries. Whenever he is not busy researching and writing, he loves to go on road trips with his wife and two children.